The Gods We Worship Live Next Door

THE AGHA SHAHID ALI PRIZE IN POETRY

THE GODS WE WORSHIP LIVE NEXT DOOR

Bino A. Realuyo

THE UNIVERSITY OF UTAH PRESS
Salt Lake City

The Agha Shahid Ali Prize in Poetry
Series Edited by Katharine Coles

 The Defiance House Man colophon is a registered trademark of the
University of Utah Press. It is based upon a four-foot-tall, Ancient
Puebloan pictograph (late PIII) near Glen Canyon, Utah.

09 08 07 06 05   5 4 3 2 1

LIBRARY OF CONGRESS CATALOGING-IN-PUBLICATION DATA

Realuyo, Bino A.
  The gods we worship live next door / Bino A. Realuyo.
    p. cm.
  "The Agha Shahid Ali Prize in Poetry."
  ISBN-13: 978-0-87480-861-2 (pbk. : alk. paper)
  ISBN-10: 0-87480-861-8 (pbk. : alk. paper)
  I. Title.
PS3568.E263G63 2006
811'.54—dc22

                    2006000183

For the Filipino people

Contents

V.

VI.

The Gods We Worship Live Next Door

I. DIASPORA: FIVE MILLION

{Over five million Filipinos work overseas,
many as maids in Europe, the Middle East, and
wealthier Asian nations, sending back seven billion
dollars to their families in the Philippines.}

Filipineza

In the modern Greek dictionary, the word "Filipineza"
means "maid."

If I became the brown woman mistaken
for a shadow, please tell your people I'm a tree.
Or its curling root above ground, like fingers without a rag,

without the buckets of thirst to wipe clean your mirrorlike floors.
My mother warned me about the disappearance of Elena.
But I left her and told her it won't happen to me.

The better to work here in a house full of faces I don't recognize.
Shame is less a burden if spoken in the language of soap and stain.
My whole country cleans houses for food, so that

the cleaning ends with the mothers, and the daughters
will have someone clean for them, and never leave
my country to spend years of conversations with dirt.

When I get up, I stand like a tree, feet steady, back firm.
From here, I can see Elena's island, where she bore a child
by a married man whose floors she washed for years,

whose body stained her memory until she left in the thick
of rain, unseen yet now surviving in the uncertain tongues
of the newly arrived. Like the silence in the circling motions

of our hands, she becomes part myth, part mortal, part soap.

Singapore Sunday

In memoriam, Mrs. Flor Contemplacion

We smooth the church courtyard
with a blanket of fried fish,
salted eggs, rice flattened in Tupperware.
No chopsticks, we say. Our mouths
long for the feel of forks and spoons.
Paper plates swiftly tumble with the wind
but only our eyes chase after them.
We laugh at the thought
of smelling like fish once again.
We all smell of newly washed plates.
Ants approach in hills of red.
I sweep them off with my fingers.
One woman looks at me, tells me,
my hands—*as natural as brooms.*
Suddenly, a shower of leaves.
Like rain, they escape from my fingers.
In our country, rain comes in the shape of leaves.
How quickly rain disappears here
through unclogged sewers.
The feel of week-old floods is unknown.
I edge away from the group and rest,
a month's worth of letters on my lap.
Leaning against a tree, I read one.
The voice of my husband waits in my ear.
A flood of breeze turns green.
Now, I don't think of Mondays.

---

*Flor Contemplacion (1953–1995) was hanged in Singapore City for killing
a fellow Filipino maid and a Singaporean boy. Many Filipinos believed that
she was framed and accused the Philippine government of not doing enough
to help her.*

Amsterdam Canal

Out there are boats, Sunday boats
but not the ones I imagined them to be.

They sail here without thinking
of a catch, of empty plates,

of fish salted quickly to last for days.
Back home, I had once waited for a boat.

One night it arrived, rusty, peeling on its side,
painted with a name I couldn't read

with faces I still remember.
Planks of wood slammed against the dock.

I rushed in, slept through smashing waves.
The nameless boat that took me

brought me here,
this city of salmon carts endlessly rolling by.

Salmon is not fish.

Not the same fried
salted milkfish in a flat rimmed basket,

banana leaves covering, to keep the flies away.
It is not deboned milkfish over steamy white rice;

cut, sliced, dipped in bowls
of vinegar and raw peppers

so hot it prickled on the tongue.
Smoked salmon in jars is not fish.

They don't hold the scent of letters on my reed mat,
which I cut open with a dry seaweed.

Letters from the farm,
Little remnants of a river crumble as they unfold.

A Night in Dubai

"How did the world revolve in this way?"

—Fadwa Tuquan

for Sarah Balabagan

The moon is veiled again and I'm afraid. The stillness smells like oil, burning at night. I sleep with the smell of my own fears, wrapped in white linen, as if he couldn't see me beyond this covering and the walls of this jail, from the walls of his grave. His eyes—observant, discontent, and aged by years of thirst—will always be open despite death. I don't remember killing him. But I remember his smell: the oil he rubbed on his body every day, the lamp he carried like jewelry at night, the burning incense as if every day he was preparing for his grave. The oil, the scent of oil, its approach as I scrubbed tile after tile of intricate squares and circles, a garden of tiles, this garden of blood and crime, even then, each tile was a memory of returning to leaves and air, pond water. In the next five days, I will be lashed a hundred times. If it means that for every lash, I will remember less, then let them do it. I will not ask for forgiveness; I will only ask for a moment to hold my mother. She is around me somewhere, behind these walls, beyond this city of cloth and eyes. She waits to take me home. She is showing my photographs to strangers who have never heard of me. I know. She is telling them: *My daughter, she is innocent, see this picture, this is my Sarah, see her smiles, she is strong, they can whip her all day, but she'd come back flying, like birds,* like seasonal birds returning to the south of our farm.

Sarah Balabagan was a 16-year-old Filipino maid in the United Arab Emirates when she was sentenced to death in 1994 for killing her 85-year-old employer, who had raped her at knifepoint. After lobbying efforts by European and Philippine groups, the sentence was reduced to a fine of $40,000, a one-year prison term, and 100 lashings.

II. SPAIN (1565–1898)

{"Will it be calm by tomorrow when we wake?
Or will we wake at all?"}*

*From "The Storm," by Ricaredo Demetillo

In the late eighteenth century, Spain, in an effort to build the Philippine economy, transformed rice fields into sugarcane plantations.

In 1796, Nathaniel Bowditch, an American, brought back four hundred tons of Philippine sugar to the U.S., marking the first significant contact between the two countries.

Azúcar

i.

Every day, I hear the chopping of canes, this tall, thin growth of thorny leaves we have never seen before. The wind sounds different here. The water in the ground doesn't speak. The canes are always drinking water. I am astounded by how quickly rice fields are replaced by these walls that never sway. Rice stalks always bow with the wind at the sight of women singing. You can't see the next person beside you; you can only hear his axe and the drip of his sweat. I am always chewing canes, no wonder ants crawl on my legs, smelling the sugar in my blood. The harvest of canes showers like arrows around us. In a few weeks, there will be another parade of canes on our shoulders, weighing down the many years we have lived here, a trail of slow-walking shadows, footprints deepening each hour, toward ships waiting at the shore. Centuries are mapped on our backs, lines perhaps of the many names we have handed down the years: my father died here, his brothers died here, all fallen, backs bent, and blood as sweet as what buried them. Sugar sweetens with each body that falls. Everybody falls. Where this sugar will go, we will never know. We don't eat sugar here; rice doesn't taste the same with sugar. Sugar sweetens with every rice field that is burned.

In the twenty-first century the Philippines, a traditionally rice-growing land, imports rice from neighboring countries.

ii.

Amid noise of cement trucks,
soil is bulldozed into a new road.
The sugarcanes have dried,
like me, thinning even.
I was once the stalk you chewed,
pulp fed to thirst, after a long day,
the hours in my long hair,
the softness between rough teeth.

Watch these footprints dry up in mud;
listen to them crack, split—
even my own do as I walk away.
The sun is with me again,
and the child,
whose thirst is like yours.
But in spite of open eyes, I dream
about you again:

back bent in the field, stabbing skin of canes,
awaiting the approach of my feet:
the music of dry bark, a baby on my back,
the scent of a basket of rice and fish.
The baby was wailing then as he does now.
He has always been thirsty,
always yelling my name, his first word,
your last—

A truckload of canes drove beside you.
The trucker didn't look in the mirror,
at my open mouth,

the basket's tumble in the air.
He would never know
I still think about it now, seeing again
and again—sugarcanes sliding over,
burying you with leaves.

Sultan Kudarat

*"Powerful is not he who knocks the other down, indeed
powerful is he who controls himself in a fit of anger."*

—from the *Hadith*, a collection of sayings
by the prophet Muhammad

Legend is a memory that arises from simple truths,
a white cloak and century-old swords
for the next communion with skin.
We are tired now, old. There is barely food here to nourish
our legends, no lands to carry the weight of water and seeds.
There is no fish. In an island without them, the air
we breathe is not the same. Look around: empty forests,
burnt mosques, cracked and discolored arches.
The odor of guns and grease, abandoned flesh.
Our children are lost too, as much as yours.
You may not know. We named them after legends
we tried to remember. Now that they are gone,
our legends have passed with them, unlike the names
of your people, taken after each country that took your hand,
from every mouth that drooled over your skin.
Your cathedral bells ring in this island where they don't belong.
Much does not belong here: our fates, our plight, and these bells
that echo the screams of those buried underneath the marble floors,
those sunk in soil that is not ours anymore.
We are not about temples and mosques.
Silent prayers hardly keep the day. Each time you kneel
to pray, we kneel to touch our graves,
these stones through which you planted crosses so deep
they clogged the open mouths of our dead.

Procession

In memoriam, Father Narciso Pico, human rights activist

Air descends in spirals. On a street,
a flock waits, not in usual Sunday white
but black, a long line, spiraling as well.
Their sweat you can't see.
Their faces would make you wonder what really
matters to them—the wait or the destination,
something you often asked: the now or what comes next?
In this village, whoever dares ask that question
does it in murmurs, in twists of fingers,
like their ears and eyes, attentive to every house
they pass: who still lives there, who doesn't,
what's gone, what remains, their names, mentioned
every time they think of yours.
They recognize the thoughts behind fallen lips,
sunken skin: *where does a dead priest go,
the one gunned down for leaves and soil—*
tell them, if not, they would simply guess, if there is an
opening in the sun, then there, into its eye, to watch
shovels rise above the ground, your own, the sprinkle
of soil over your casket, of dust, prayers, and names,
once again, the names of those who will fall next to you.

Pagsanjan Falls, a mythical natural attraction in Luzon, has become a major destination for pedophiles from western countries.

Discovery of Skin

for F. Magellan, navigator, landed in the Philippines, beheaded, 1521

i. 1521

Sailing with lamp-lit maps, searching for voices by naming waves, you imagined: tongues on brown nipples, language deciphered through moans, sweat sliding onto shores.

Mira, tierra, mira.

We offered you fruits, rituals, primitive wishes, a dance around fire, loin-cloth smiles, but you wanted more: to unearth boys and skins, to convert our moons into crosses.

Tranquilo, indios, tranquilo.

Pebbles cut brown flesh. His thin frame bounced on soil. Breathing dried his blood. And youlifted his ankles to create shadows of legs, feet, origins of sin on his face.

In the name of the father, and of the son,
you discovered his insides.

ii. 2001

They were all there: shadows walking behind you, still, centuries past. We will never know their names, we never did, not that we never asked, but theirs were words we couldn't say, lips we couldn't read, even now: we utter nothing, so they will let us close our eyes when they feed us their bodies.

It is the money that they bring, the few coins that keep the day without fears, allowing the absence of hunger, for a few hours it would matter, for a few hours we would forget who we once were. Here, we have many words for hunger, one of them is our imitation of their fingers, white ones, thick and hairy, of the different ways of touching, touching men like them in the rain, in the waterfalls, in the lake while they float and the lotion on their skin separates away. And we watch them, and retrace the rivers back to the past: our stories, as small as our bodies, always end with your name buried in the ground. The other names for hunger are buried in the ground. When they come, they bring you back with them, soil after soil, ship after ship, the same old faces appear, the same voices we hear once again, except that now they come in many tongues, in different apparitions of history and fear.

iii. 1521

You stroked the water of his lips, sucked every pore.
"Let me be—," he begged, his mouth full of your throbbing sins. You parted his legs then asked for more.

Blessed is he who
comes
in the name of the Lord.

Hosanna in the Highest.

His savage eyes stared into the centuries ahead.
There was nothing there but noises in the language of wine, red as your eyelids, once fallen to stare at the brown of his chest.

So here once again is our ceremony of blood and flesh:
the moisture of your lips landed on his neck, his axe pounded on yours, your head was left to bounce on your discovered land.

In the name of the Holy Spirit,
your blood splattered on your soul.

III. U.S.A (1898–1946)

{"Shall we? That is, shall we go on conferring our Civilization upon the peoples that sit in darkness, or shall we give those poor things a rest."}*

*From "To the Person Sitting in Darkness," by Mark Twain

1899

The Forgotten Leaf

*"We never left one alive. If one was wounded
we would run our bayonets though him."*

—An American soldier,
Philippine-American war, 1901

He left me clinging to life, my body laid bare over thousands of others, arms an open cross, a fallen embrace to hold what were: faces kissing earth, a pile of dry leaves, decomposing wall of bodies, but finally— free. Was death, this time, god's gift? To die in the name of god, and to not know the names of those whom you see him with; they were all staring at each other, limbs intertwined, some with tears of blood, others, spit, but all dead, and their names, no, they had none; but for many years to come, it would not matter if they did. Who would remember them, and me? Who would remember me on my knees, begging, and this soldier, thrusting through my mouth fifty years of *Juan-to-John*? Who could tell my face from others in a fading photograph? Time had a way of forgetting. People had a way of letting time forget. My people: they forgot me the moment my body was thrown up the hill. Did anyone know I left children? Did my children know how I died? Did they know that my body was buried in the same soil on which they strode? I was the tree that grew from it, the hibiscus blooming at dusk, the roots, the memorial of pebbles and dust, the old amputee sitting in his shadow, the glue-children begging for a few coins. Did anyone know my name? In museums, you would find the bayonets that killed me, etched with the years on which they struck. The shadow of blood held still, reminiscing the faces that created it. So if in a photograph you saw my face, if at your touch its yellowing paper peeled, think of me, a country had once fallen, and I went along with it, in death, in life, yet always, forgotten.

U.S. military bases in the Philippines were officially closed in 1992. Departing American servicemen left behind more than 30,000 unacknowledged children born to Filipino girlfriends and bar girls.

Consummatum Est

(It is finished)

i.

Only a child's cry can bring me back
to this: a small rented room, the scent
of folded uniforms, starch-pressed

nights before, the cutting sound
of zippers, luggage sagging on his shoulders,
her weight kicking in my womb.

The child's hair wasn't like mine,
not as dark as his tattoo of my hair.
Her eyes: she had eyes of leaves,

a fan of leaves in the summer.
On a storm of leaves, I gave her away.
I heard she was named Luna.

She was light as sun.
I think of the half-child returning.
She will wonder for a moment

what could have been: fields of grain, a river,
a father. Instead, a landfill of ash,
ruins of dimly-lit rooms.

Once, I was the woman soaked in sweat.

A man was flinging dollars onto my bed.
His luggage rolled on the waxed wooden floor.

And the doors, the chaotic memory of doors—

ii.

The boy twists inside a huge cement pipe.
His skin rubs against a floor of rain,
where heads of lizards crawl over for air,

roach sacs crack underfoot.
He thinks of how long his body
can last curved, legs bent, head bowed.

In the serenity of dripping mud,
voices circle his arms,
children who always ridicule his hair:

so kinky and brittle it breaks,
knuckles so dark darker than theirs.
Only insects drown in the dark.

While hours drip from chin to chest,
he dreams of finding his mother.
He will not ask, nor expect her to tell why

she gave him away, but he will say
one thing: how halfway through his life
he looked like his father,

the last half, he will look like her.

---

*"Consummatum Est:" The alleged last words of Jose P. Rizal, national hero of
the Philippines before he was shot by a firing squad in 1896, two years before
Spain surrendered to the U.S. to end the Spanish-American war.*

GI Baby

All is memory, its guise in grass tufts, stone piles
and low voices. All in memory is a landscape: barbed wires
that crown this vast open space, a multitude of metal parts,
grease cans and children picking them all day.

This is harvest: to walk there, and make one wrong step,
time sometimes explodes; bodies bury themselves in the air.
But that is the cheapest way to die? she thinks. Vaporize?
A drizzle of blood? So what? How much do coffins cost these days?

She belongs here. At ten, she has cut barbed wires, cleared trails,
so she can come and go. "GI Maria," the children call her.
Once, they asked why her eyes had the color of rust,
to watch her face turn red. Red, the way brown skin doesn't.

It is her finding that makes her different, the third sense.
The way she spots metal that sells quickly.
Something left in her blood, just like everything else: the
empty buildings around, the taste of oil on skin, light eyes, hair,

even lighter, and her last name that no one can ever say.
Enough that her face reminds them of the Stateside years.
Enough that it is why she was left like the note of her name,
an abandoned page of a day, a memory that crawls

to her like the tales of a forgotten war, lust and landscape.

IV. JAPAN (WORLD WAR II: 1942-1946)

{"Your death has never been in a grave in any country, anywhere."}*

*From "Standing Coffin," by Ryuichi Tamura

Pantoum: The Comfort Woman

*for Mrs. Rosa Henson, the first Filipina woman to accept
Japanese reparation payment for her suffering as a comfort
woman for Japanese soldiers in a brothel for nine months
during World War II.*

Monsoon country, so expectedly, wind uproots memory.
Rain is the voice of a storyteller, one without pause
like my nightly return to the hundred days of bulb light
and curtains, laughter and weight of soldiers outside, lined up.

Rain, tell me the story once again; mine, don't pause—
sounds of belts unbuckle, dawn; blood gorges to a rush downward.
Let me weigh their laughter one by one, past rooms of curtains,
where my body tilts, reaching out, upward, tied to a post

with a belt, the dawn of memory, the rush of sound:
"Tanaka—," I scream. My husband awakens, "Who is he—Tanaka?"
My body tilts upward, reaching you, untying a dream.
Tanaka, my dear, he and the darkness are one, always waiting

and awake, a whisper at night, a husband to his wife, a soldier
to me, a Japanese soldier without a choice, breathing through limbs.
Tanaka in the darkness was as dear as the wait to escape.
Tanaka in the morning was as cruel as the smell of his peers,

these Japanese whose choices were my limbs, mouth, and breath.
I never told you, my dear, that every night, I leave my hands beside you
to carry the rest back to the cruelty of their smell, of their mornings:
nine months of war in this hut, my body as food, my life as nothing.

If I tell you how it was, will you hold my hands, surrender to memory?
Soon I will disappear, running naked in a hut, pursued by ropes,
    shadows.

Nine months: a war for the rest of my life, for the rest of nothing,
telling the rain, the wind, voices of storytellers, ones without pause,

how I disappeared to be naked as rope, naked as its shadow,
in this hut of fears, hands limp and tied, slipping into thoughts;
I told the rain to carry my voice, the wind to hold it without pause.
Now, in my monsoon country, so expectedly, wind uproots memory.

1942

The War Haiku

Flood of bullet shells.
In the rain, you hear the last
evening of the war.

*

A charcoal city.
Once the brown of reed mat roofs,
whistling walls of grass.

*

Barracks doors open.
You: bloated, muddy, almost blind.
Air pulls bodies out.

*

Scratches on walls.
Years of darkness written in
finger-scraped lines.

*

"He looks like he's dead."
A woman places her ear
on your rib-thin chest.

*

Bayonet scars
map weeks of torture and sun.
"He is still breathing."

*

A city sees again,
much clearer than your eyes,
cataracts removed.

*

You multiply moons
in narrow white V.A. halls,
talking to yourself.

Every year, hundreds of young Filipino women are recruited to work as "cultural entertainers" in Japan, often becoming victims of prostitution and rape.

Japayuki

Amid sand and broken shells lost around her feet,
the wait had begun. Fishing boats were pulled ashore,

fathers inside, paddling, bodies as stiff as oars;
their scent was a night's catch of dead fish.

A collection of little boats, light as paper,
heavy as water receding from shore.

She baptized them, with cupped hands—
Fe, Esperanza, Caridad—then wore them:

a necklace of three little boats on beads
of seashells. Someday, a string of pearls.

Or a string of pearly combs, a gift
to the mother who did the perpetual combing

of her hair, who taught her about simplicity
with each strand that fell on her lap.

*Don't wish for more than fried fish on your plates
or more than the aluminum plates themselves.*

Porcelain, she preferred; she could lick it off clean.
Chicken bones and pork never got caught in the throat.

She was tired of fish and the litany of hours:
the daily wait for fathers with fish,

the endless counting of moons, the sewing of fishnets
on hot afternoons, the threading of seashells to sell—

only to witness a drowned catch of dead men.
So why not more?

Because here,
nothing is more.

A boat out to the sea at nineteen. Her mother waved goodbye,
her skin felt like fishscales, body sprinkled with salt:

How far are you going?
Isn't it too far for you? From me?

Yes. But that was a country where everything was hope.
Neon-lit country, yens of hope, eaters of raw fish.

Everybody was talking about it. All young women went there,
sing, dance, they would do all that: "O genki desu ka?"

Little paperboats in a girl's cupped palm...
a young woman floats in the cupped palm of a dead sea.

In memoriam, Maricris Sioson

From a Filipino Death March Survivor Whose World War II Benefits Were Rescinded by the U.S. Congress in 1946

In Memoriam, Augusto Roa Realuyo, 1921–2003

1. I left three years ago.
2. If you want to know about my rural childhood, ask my survivors.
3. If you want to know how I was recruited into the United States army at twenty, ask President Roosevelt.
4. If you want to know how I ended up in the Death March at twenty-one, ask General MacArthur.
5. If you want to know how many of my friends perished in the Japanese concentration camps, ask General Homma.
6. If you want to know how I contracted malaria, beri-beri, dysentery, skin disease, gastrointestinal disease in one month, ask the Japanese Camp Commander.
7. If you want to know how my military benefits were rescinded at the end of the war, ask President Truman.
8. If you want to know how I became a 100% disabled veteran, ask my V.A. doctors.
9. If you want to know how I got burial benefits, ask President Clinton.
10. If you want to know why I wasn't buried in Arlington, ask Judge Owen.
11. If you want to know how I died without seeing the Rescission Act of 1946 repealed, ask me again.
12. Then again.
13. I've been asking myself the same question for sixty years.

14. _____.

15. I don't know why, really.

16. I don't know why Filipinos have ignored it for so long.

17. I don't know why Americans don't know this happened.

18. I don't want to think about this anymore.

19. 46...

20. 06. Sixty years. I couldn't wait anymore.

At the end of World War II the U.S. Congress passed the Rescission Act of 1946, which denied Filipino veterans wartime benefits. Filipino veterans of World War II, now in their twilight years, continue to fight for their dignity and the benefits owed to them.

V. WITNESS

{"You whom I could not save

Listen to me.

Try to understand this simple speech as I would be ashamed of another.

I swear, there is in me no wizardry of words.

I speak to you with silence like a cloud or a tree."}*

*From "Dedication," by Czeslaw Milosz

Witness

"The silence. The silence.
The silence covers everything."

—Teresa de Jesus

In this town, everybody bends all morning,
to bury an acre of fear each hour, to feed
the ground with all the words they will not say.

Another man was found last week: caned,
powdered, tied with grass.
She was there: crawling on mud, hiding

behind a rock and spires of grass,
and days later, hiding from the memory
of faces and voices: the foundered glint of a man

in the sun, the broken words, wound upon wound,
the thin blur of those around him, their laughter,
the whippings, their tight grasp of their whips—

Is to speak of this to finally forget?
To speak of it is to know that so much here
remains hidden—the silence, the air,

all inhaled, kept inside, food for fear.
At twilight, dogs begin to bark. Broken twigs,
bullets, and shadows flee between trees.

Not again. She cups her mouth, hoping
that there is no spill of blood, parts of limbs
scratching soil. She firmly holds herself,

latches the door with wood, tight as teeth.
Night seeps through bullet holes on the walls,
sits with her while she listens, wilting, on a chair.

Cotabato, Philippines

Glue Children

i. Night

There is no odor of dog droppings.
Starry-eyed children sleepwalk in the smog.
One boy pees in his pants then cradles
his plastic bag of glue, as if to mother
a child and his desires, like the day
when his streetname was first given to him,
after pickpocketing a bystander, slashing
skin. Another cups a half-empty can,
then buries his face in its mouth.
He possesses its aroma, the way he
would his fantasy mother: *I will hold
her arms, never let her go.* No moments
to waste: they sniff away the cruelty
of meanings, disappearing in its thickness.

ii. Day

Wiping the dirt off her face, she adds more.
The sun shows it all: the yellowing eyes,
hollow skin, dust lines as intricate as streets.
If asked, she will not tell you her age.
Seven, a friend once said. He could tell by her
voice, the innocent sloping of curses—all of which
she knows by now—a mirror of fast tongues,
of hungry feet ringed by worms and rain.
Eight perhaps, but that is most. She wonders
which of her fingers is eight, counting them
over and over, like the empty bottles found
in the dump, for which she got a peso bill.
A-one, a-two, a-three. She smiles so rarely
for a child, born every morning, dead every night.

iii. Night

Cardboard boxes unfold, bodies sprawl
the sidewalk city, illuminated by lamps
and the occasional spill of siren lights.
She dives, this littlest one, under a thick rag
in an empty corner, then watches closely
as the night whisks by: women in stockings,
the parade of manicured skirts and fingers,
car windows lowering with blistered smiles,
old men wheeling stares at the eclipse of hands.
Beyond, the horizon sets the customary descent
of children curling under its vesperal breath,
bones covered with boxed rags. And she wonders,
cheek pressed against her cardboard bed,
which fingernail is blue, which is red.

Queen

They hook tin cans, glass, and bottles.
Baskets bigger than them,
tied around their backs.
Go there, commands the girl, *up there,*
her hair, oil-flattened, crowned with tin foil.
She orders her soldiers to climb
where their kingdom meets the sky.
Stateside food up there! She raises her voice.
Her display of authority satisfies
a week-long craving for rice.
Soon they move out of their nests like flies,
winged with a natural flair for quest,
fleeing through smoky curves, leaping,
landing on their stick-thin limbs
on these many hills of garbage.
She leads masterfully, armed
with a steel hook and stolen rubber boots.
There, she is above the wideness of earth,
which she wraps with open arms and fingers.
She smiles. First, she will divide this kingdom
among the hungriest shadows
until almost nothing is smelled or seen.
And then, with her mouth, she will create another:
one with gardens of charcoal-broiled fish
and hills of simmering white rice.

Flower Vendor

Always, the beginning is in the wetting
of the thread at its tip.
It won't take long—and she knows—
to make necklaces of white flowers.
A wired bulb swings above her,
splashing shadows of arms, hair,
and flowers in buckets.

She sits at the mirror and revels
in another day of yelling:
the stretching of words for flowers
hanging around her neck, wrists,
the wide leaps amid loud honking buses
and mouths, and the narrow ones over puddles,
the balance of an umbrella if it rains
while wiping her forehead with her hand,
the quick count of change
between the drivers' shouts and whistles.

The rain of hours drifts through her dress.
She breathes in mounds of scent around her.
The reed-mat ceiling slowly drips.
She counts the drips as she exhales,
tongues her lips to begin.

Brownout

At night, the light goes out.
Old men gather the remainders

of light with candles in their hands,
necklaces of garlic and talk of tales:

women in flowing white silk,
half-bodied matrons with a taste for the unborn,

mother-spirits who walk amongst us.
But you know better than to search for horror in the afterlife.

The living should only fear the living,
you whisper in my ear. *The dead can't touch us.*

So you begin to brave my contours,
looking for the quickest way in.

Candlelight landscapes my breasts.
Mosquitoes feast on your skin.

The room of walls watches, its mouth
wide open, our bodies in its throat.

My fingers spider around your beast,
but I am listening to ghost stories outside,

ghosts who have a body like mine,
not yours, never a thick one like yours.

I think of how my waist may just cleave
while you water it with your tongue,

How my tongue may grow long, hairy,
coiling and splitting at the tip

to taste you, slurp you inside,
until you find yourself in my waters.

So this is how it always begins: these last hours of my womb,
the conception of fear.

The Leaning Tenement of Taytay

"The tenement units that deposed president Joseph Estrada built for his supporters from San Juan, Metro Manila, are falling apart."

—Philippine Daily Inquirer

Yet this is no Leaning Tower, no *Seventh Wonder of the World,*
a wonder for your eyes maybe, or for your noses.
How can you not smell the approach of wind,
its spiral push downward, into you? What you cannot see

is the architecture of the missing: the water in faucets
and pipes, the light to bring fireflies to nights, the smiles.
Where is the simplicity of windows and doors, the way out
should we fall, the way in when it rains, cracked roofs for cover?

In our structure of wonder, we wait, then forget.
Inside it, inside us, there are no more rooms to rest the blame,
no time to find anger, and there is plenty of that—anger—
the whole of it so inside the hidden inside.

We don't think of it or him: he who listened, half-built. Half-tried.
The trying keeps our voices muted, so he doesn't know he's our hero
somewhat. No one has even taken us there, even halfway—trying
    is hard
if it means lending a hand to those who have tried a lifetime of tries.

Soon, our half-built home will come down. Every day, it shakes
as people drive by to look. Still, we hold many things whole: our
    breaths,
our prayers, our names. So goes another day of leaning our bodies
against the wall, and another night of eyelids shut with fear:

that split-second scream of daylight, half rubble, half dream.

Because Yesterday
I Jumped Out of a Plane

"In what turned out to be a bizarre and even comic drama yesterday, a Philippine Airlines jet with 278 passengers and 13 crew members was hijacked by a man who, armed with a hand grenade and a gun, robbed the passengers and later jumped out of the plane while it was flying over Antipolo."

—Philippine Daily Inquirer

A dream of flying. At the edge of our world, a wish to grow wings. At the sight of the heavens, envy, pure, permanent. Why do clouds move with such ease and grace? Why do nights reveal stars that fail to grant our wishes? Come look our way. People who ask my mother why I hijacked and parachuted from a plane should stay here a day to see what it's like. The news crew came, heavy with cameras, paper, and questions, because you really ought to know. Never long enough to stay near a sewer and look around. Our lives are shadowed by clotheslines. Our street signs are the drunks at the corner bends, a giant maze littered with desires for love that never came. Our children run around laughing; their cries no longer convince anyone of their hunger. Is it so disturbing that I boarded a plane and held it up for a thousand pesos? That wouldn't buy a day's meal as we know it? When I opened the door and jumped to my death, I knew on the other side I would learn how to fly. How light I felt then. Yet wingless still. Learning how to float, to become one with wind and death. Oh, death. Death has many reasons for being—what I could never explain then, I know now. So the next time you look at the skies and find something speeding your way, think of a falling star. Make another wish, your first one perhaps? It could very well be me visiting again. I will listen to you. Whisper in your ears the reasons why you should grow wings on land. The way there are many reasons why death is meant to be.

The Pepper-Eater

"Guinness Book of [World] Record Stays with Filipino Pepper Eater"

—Philippine Daily Inquirer

An old man lost for not having a complete set of teeth.
Another for having Maalox after downing 550 pieces.

But I had 650 peppers! More than anyone! said another.
Hot! I said, but knew better: the man never chewed, only swallowed!

Pepper in the mouth is my quickest picker upper *(when I'm down)*.
A pepper a day keeps the town-healer away *(all males anyhow)*.

Unpeel the green, red, the in-between, all 350!, popping,
scorching, dancing colorful world records in my mouth.

Oh, this flavor, this life! If sweetness reveals the fruit,
our character hangs on the burning flesh of bulbous peppers.

Think of my city in the south, and watch the hot-tempered men,
exposed torsos all day, hungry for a night of peppery-itch.

Swing another way and smell the women who fan their insides
with burning eyes and lips. These are no ordinary women.

Have you heard of our volcano, its perfect cone? It erupts
and CNN comes to cover it. This is no ordinary town.

No wonder God makes constant visits.
All the men here become priests, the women whores.

I go to neither one. I'm just a world-class pepper-eater.

Lunar Eclipse

"We don't know how many people were on each ship."

—A navy spokesman on the collision of a container
ship and an inter-island ferry in Manila Bay

The sun at night.

You hope to see nothing
with your eyelids fallen.

Around you, bones of earth are revealed,
sap of wood like blood, leaks.

What you don't see, you smell.
So fearful, everything, everything.

A walk midstream.
An open space. Nothing here is hidden.

Do you wish to float?
Do you wish to walk on water?

Mama ...

Bodies, the stones of sea, steadily float,
skin reminiscing what once was water full of life.

Flesh smells like the insides of air,
once opened in the rain.

Thirst, impossible.
You are so afraid, always so.

Waves fall facing away from you,
ripping one child then his mother, water midstream.

The moon at night.

234 people were reported dead while 85 persons remained missing after they were buried by tons of garbage at the Payatas dumpsite in Metro Manila, home to more than 60,000 squatters.

Find Me

Out bursts my right hand, climbing the freedom of air.
My left almost made it, but it hits the inside of a huge empty can.
The rest of me is stuck deep in this cemetery of dirt.

Oh, take   *me*—

Away from my familiar, the stench of the everyday.
At my last memory now: last night's avalanche of wails left me sinking
against a limbless stranger on whom my chances rest.

Find me. Pull me out. Clean my shattered skin. Return to me my name.
I am *one* of you, one of *you*, deserving of a resting place in soil,
of parting words in stone.

Of a memorial for a death half-lived.

Focus, and catch the shape of my arm in charred pipes, blood, soot.
Come quietly—to the north of Mt. Payatas, where once stood a shanty
    I made myself.
Where women dug for pieces of dreams in metal sheets, cans,

and worm-infested foods. What we called ours was ours, our bodies
    marking
the northern garbage dump, away from the brutes who made a killing
    killing,
all of us buried just the same.

Does it matter now who owed whom what?

Our story smells thick, it's suspicious. Your questions, even thicker,
mostly punctuated with blame. They begin for you today,
questions ending with questions ending with our faces, the way it
  has been,

the way it has always been—us: conversation pieces, the soil of your
  shame,
the inspiration for your movies. A quiet interlude to sympathy.
Mouths open as you watch TV news, as you gather your thoughts
  in shock:

Look, we made CNN again.

Thanks to a country that mends torn limbs with names of saints:
Let's leave it to the Lord, you say, sweet whispers, you turn your
  head away.
I'm wearing your dirt, every thread of it, come smell.

Big flies finally find me, then the dogs. Birds. My family of hunger.
I have yet to see humans, the ones in gloves and plastic helmets.
Nostrils covered, eyes exposed. *We're afraid no one has survived.*

I know when I stopped breathing.

I see when I began to float.

I don't know where I'm heading, where to touch the light that will
  take me there.

I call out names of friends, and no one hears my voice but me.

I smell the sunset's red stare.

I see the faces rise from our fallen mountain, one by one, red shadows.

I hear the emergency men descend down the ashes, red crosses.

I smell all of us, all there now, standing once again.

I look back at my circle of life: my right arm sinks, my left, into the womb of your trash, deep in a cemetery with no soil, no crosses, no names, and always, no heart.

I.

Cycles

*"Only her of whom I think: You
I cannot see."*
                    —Rainer Maria Rilke

i. Death: the night following

Fireflies buzz over candlelight.
A child counts them, then folds her fingers between
her knees. Everything is so still, yet tentative:
her sleepless gaze, the moon's shadows, bare feet.

She does not surrender. She has not forgotten
what her father once said: when there are fireflies, spirits roam,
before the dead's remains are cushioned by dirt, leaves, petals,
before they are watered by wails and crosses.
Spirits stand still, even the Book says forty days.
They sit on twigs, between.

Light in the shape of fins swims in the night, waits
for the moment she catches its flicker, its body,
scales of blue fire and flesh.
But she waits for spirits, a chance to see them when the wind
is caught between leaves. Papa, she calls. *Come back.*
In any form: a glimmer, a vision, the smell of air and cigars,
of his morning skin.

Papa, sit with me. Tell me the story of the moon.

Trees add shadow, clouds darkness. Everything is heavy here.
Irreversible. Except this flame that continues to burn wings,
so delicately waxes firefly after firefly,
then molds them into a sculpture of ashen parts.

ii. Life: the day preceding

Candlewax ripples like a pond on a drizzle, then it blurs, hardens. If tears can do the same, the next time they come will be worth waiting for. Nobody here waits anymore (what you always say), not even trees. Water does not come so often, and never in its best form, rain. When the bullets kiss your pores, you wonder about that moment: the last jump of blood out of your skin, the pinch of breath. You lie there, talk to trees until this woman finds you. She brings with her the smell of sulphur. Always that same smell when someone is anointed and confessed. You whisper to her and for once do not ask the name of a woman you have just met. *You smell like a candle?* Light opens in the sky. There is a house of spirits above us all. Candles on stairs, on marble treads. She places your head on her middle. *Is that a pillow?* A child, she responds, on her ninth month. Inside all of us, there has always been a child. Yours has been killed many times. Even she can tell by the way she looks at you. But she doesn't ask who you are—a rebel, a convict, a lover? This is the pinnacle of your ninth life: your ears on her mound where life kicks within, then the final thoughts—a name, a name for a child who will one day bring rain.

VI. THE GODS WE WORSHIP LIVE NEXT DOOR: A POEM IN ELEVEN PARTS

{"Our gods die one by one and caskets golden
Are borne on the hard pavements at even
Down roads named after them, across the plains
Where all gods go. Oh, we outlive them all
But there are junior gods fast growing tall."}*

*From "The Gods We Worship Live Next Door," by Bienvenido Santos

"Clashes continued in Mindanao between Islamist secessionist groups and the AFP. Serious human rights abuses, including unlawful killings, committed by government forces and opposition armed groups continued in the context of these conflicts. Harassment, killings, or 'disappearances' of opposition politicians, activists, and journalists were also reported. Reports of torture and ill-treatment of criminal suspects by police, including rape and sexual assault of female prisoners and mistreatment of children, highlighted deficiencies in the administration of justice."

—Amnesty International, 2003

i. Mother and child

Mama, I'm thirsty . . .

The mother washes clothes more carefully than she would her own.
These are not hers, not even the child's.

She doesn't touch the child's clothes anymore.

The child listens in the dark, singing

but she can't hear him   he sings inside himself,
to himself.

Nobody hears this child sing.

In a bucket, her fingers
reach for a bar of diminishing soap.

There is lichen on walls.

She finds herself counting: pesos, days of the sun,
shirts, shirts, other people's shirts, how much they are worth, washed,
    dried, cleaned.

She thinks of the child. So beautiful a face to be covered by dirt.

The child whispers something she will never hear.

Nobody hears this child speak.

Once, she got up at night so she could listen to his breathing. It never
   rained on those nights; she could clearly listen to him, and in the
   dark, saw the traces of her face on his. Their eyes were most alike,
   except now. Hers are always open.

How does anyone rest in soil?

The child watches, face between folded knees —
why does lather thicken and rise, who made bubbles, the thousand
   faces in each one?

Soap slips, lather slips. The thought of the child never slips.

The child wants his hands in the lather, his face in a bubble.
He crawls slowly toward his mother, humming a song
she doesn't hear.

The mother lets the lather rise then pounds it down until a bubble
   escapes to the wind.

She rotates her head, the thickness of veins on her neck visible, her
   face, thirsty, her eyes, full of the day's endings.

Nothing begins, everything ends.

Everything.

   The child looks up. The bubble circles him.

He follows, sings.

The bubble listens.

Come.

ii. The mother

After making the sign of the cross, she kisses her thumb.

The child's picture on a table. Candles on both ends. The smell of light
overcomes fish.

A whisper.

Louder, nobody will hear you.

Another whisper, maybe his name, a face on the picture that stares
at her, identical mouths.

Most of the time, anger takes the shape of a whisper.

A mother in black.

A dry flower, long-stemmed. Not a rose but red and brittle just the
same, and the smell, as lingering.

She holds the stem, presses it, thorns meet flesh, then air, no feeling.

Slowly, above the candlelight, the table, the picture, while looking at
him still, she lifts her fingers to the wall, the wall of bullet holes.

Another line is drawn. The twentieth day.

After kissing her thumb, she says his name.

iii. The child and the bubble

> The child chases the bubble
> he doesn't see himself in it.

The bubble has its own face, not his, not his mother's.

> *Come.*

The bubble floats around him, sending off light—blue that lines his
  head, red that dots parts of his neck and yellow that melts on
  his lips.

> *Come.*

The child stares, tilts his head, pulls the tips of his hair,
slips the strands into his mouth,   eyes open, listening

Come.

> The child follows, the child hums, the bubble hums with him.

The world opens.

iv. The boy on the rock

The bubble spins in space.

Watch, the bubble says. The child opens his eyes.

There—

A quiet rendering of space—

there:
a boy climbs a rock with a face of knife-etched names.
He looks for it but he doesn't see his.
He wonders whose names they are, why even Papa's isn't there.

The child watches him.

The boy stands on a rock, bare toes feeling its pitted face. His body is
    smaller than the spires of grass.

Names.

He sees a field of grain, in the middle a lake, in the middle a face
of an old man soaked in his own bewildered eyes, shaky fingers over
    his mouth.

Papa, he screams, Papa?

Soldiers approach, big as men, or bigger, the green tide of grass
    swaying,
paddling the surface of the lake with the butts of their guns.

Papa—, he warns.

Komunista! The voices of the soldiers are louder than his,
than Papa's when he calls for his basket of lunch,
than the quick thump of the boy's feet on the rock.
But what is loudest
is the sound of arm-long guns on Papa's head,
almost like fists hitting a face, except fists don't fill half the lake with
    blood, don't make cut skin float.

Papa—

The boy jumps, runs to the lake.

Papa—

The etchings of names are left behind.

Water climbs the boy's neck, flows inside his clothes, pulls him into the
softness of soil that tickles his feet.

It isn't the soil that completely pulls him down,
or the air that screams of gunshot,
but the hands of the soldiers
on his head like palms of heavy rain,
that kind of rain that only comes at night,
until bubbles don't come out of his mouth anymore,
and his body is floating face down.

The child watches the boy's name appear on the rock.

The child watches the father and his son stare at the bottom of
the pond,
absorbing water
then air.

v. The bubble

The bubble looks at the questioning child:

Why, the child's eyes open, unflinching, why are you showing these
to me?

Komunista *is the look in a farmer's eyes when he's hungry,*
the taste in a soldier's tongue when he's bored.

Communist is when gunpowder mixes with blood.

Come. Witness more. There are more. More of them. Look—

What's there? Who is she?

vi. The watcher of the pond

Thoughts are as frequent as birds feeding their nests
even if their eggs are long gone, hatched by famished worms.

The girl's thoughts climb trees, curve around cracked shells, sometimes
    stuck
in twigs, outside, the peeled outside.

She may be a worm herself, hidden in soil, curled, especially *that* day:

        Nobody could see her, except that she could see them, all of
them, all of it happening before her eyes.

Almost: the word that saved her. They almost got me . . .

But they got *them.*

Again, the men in green. Again, that word—komunista—thrown
    at them.

She has heard it many times before. She never knew what it meant,
    komunista.

It was a morning nobody would know as if it never came. The leaves
    crackled,
the soil crackled, louder, the air crackled.

Thatched roofs, all of them the shape of coconut husks, cut in half. Everybody around them, in them, is milk, the morning pouring.

That day, they were grinding coconut meat, little hills of white in bowls. The wind could blow them off.

Sometimes, the wind is the only sound they hear. Sometimes, the meandering voyage of insects in soil.

Lips speak in secrets; every word is forgotten as soon as it is said.

The men in green: a uniform of leaves, raw and thick. They listen, always they do, and when they hear—you'd better run away.

What they heard was something else. She knew. She was there.

The wind spoke too:

Watch what you say, you never know who listens.

The slope of voices into the ground. *Komunista!* They would remain there, these voices. Nobody would ask who said what.

All there were: the sun, the marking of boots on soil, leading to the house.

Lights sprinkled, and sounds she had not heard of in her life. This place had never heard screams, cries, beggings. They were all there, sloping into the floor with their knees.

Soon, a burning roof. Thatch is only burnt to scare off bees. And often, to swing with the wind, to collect honeycombs. No bees here. Just the bitterness of bullets.

The men in green: marching, their lips, always fed, always hungry, as
    if to live forever.

Everything they left is gone.

Everything is gone.

      The pond remains, and suddenly, the disquiet in the way trees
sway, the way soil moves in waves.

Boot prints remain, a memorial to five bodies in a burnt thatched
    house.

She remains in a world that didn't stay with her. She waits and
    watches the circular patterns on the pond.

The wind smells of bodies, a perfumery of spirits, week-old flesh.

Birds fly above her, in search of eggs they can claim as their own.

vii. The mother

The mother paces inside the house: a touch on the window, a
    fingernail scratch on the wall, and at every pause, a moment to
    ponder on the child's picture, to count the days he has been gone.

The numbered days are almost gone.

In the dark of the room, she wonders whether her shadow is really
    hers.

She walks out of the house, into the street, laundry carefully wrapped
    over her head. Her shadow looks like a tree, a moving tree with
    leaves spilling into the noise.

Eyes follow her around, listening.

Flies hover, a pattern that leads to more open streets, more eyes, more puddles.

She doesn't look at anyone. She has long stopped deciphering whispers, their meanings, about whom they are said.

There are voices of children behind her. Bottlecaps are thrown into the holes on the unpaved roads.

She hears voices.

Upon hearing a certain pitch, she stops, turns, then stares at a boy squatting on a cement block. His little fingers poke into the holes of softdrink bottles, making careful sounds, so swift they are carried to her.

His feet are dirty, muddy, toes separated like open fingers after being wet by rain. His neck is thick, with lines, birth lines, and his face has a birthmark, so big it is almost a third eye, a dark lip that can't speak.

She approaches him, bends her knee to lower herself, asks for his name.

You don't look like my son, but you smell like him.

viii. The child

Where are we going now, the child asks, where are you taking me?

To a house of veils, one with pointed domes, the shape of teardrops and walls as quiet as the voices inside.

Come.

Why are they wearing those? Who are they?

ix. The children of the mosque

It is the day of the mosque, the worship of silence, the decay of colors.
  White becomes the color of the village. Even the air wears white.
  Even the air is silent.

But there is a certain smell, like raw meat on the day it's forbidden.
  Something is not supposed to be here, but *it* is here, approaching
  slowly.

The color of the sky is red. The skin of fire has peeled to rise above
  the village.

Red does not belong here.

She comes out of the mosque and sees everything unfamiliar. She is
  one of them, or she was—the women covered in white, only their
  eyes can be seen, veils over their mouths rippling when they
  breathe. What one notices most is the darkness in their eyes. What
  white can do to bring out that unspoken language.

Their eyes mourn. And that morning, everything is veiled.

She caresses her stomach. In her mind, she calls to her unborn, asks
  her if she feels the strangeness around them too.

There is something here, something, I don't know what it is, or
  where it is, but I am suddenly afraid. Tell me Allah, what is it?
  Take me there—

Moths in the field, a long twisted path of dust and dry grass. Their
     flight is low and steady, like the tide in an ocean empty of fish,
     like the clouds over an island where it seldom rains.

The sun is out, as always, the soil is as dry as her skin, as always,
     although nobody knows.

This is how it begins: the sight of her house. This is when she
     remembers: the burnt house.

The way the soldiers held their guns, almost as restless as the morning
     when they came.

You, muslim woman—, they screamed, *where is your husband?*

Inside. She pointed. Her children gathered around her, then behind
     her, all of them in white. Everyone wore garments that didn't set
     them apart.

In the eyes of the soldiers, everything there was wrong.

Komunista ka! Komunista ka! The soldiers yelled. The house was
     suddenly filled with voices of men. She couldn't tell them apart.
     She couldn't tell which voice was her husband's.

He had always been quiet, her husband, like the nights when the nets
     were filled with fish, or the nights after when they weren't.

Line up outside, all of you! The soldiers came out.

The children began to cry, all six of them. They pushed each other to
     hide inside her dress. Always this sense of knowing where to turn:
     the sun's familiarity with the mountain from which it rises, a
     mother's sudden remembrance of the thirteen years spent raising
     her children.

Don't touch them!

One by one, she felt her children's heads inside her dress. She held her stomach, as if by doing so she was keeping the unborn.

But that day, nothing was going to be kept.

We are not what you think. We are not communists! My husband is not a communist!

You muslims have always been communists! That was the last time she heard them speak. From then on, it was all her:

Don't take my children, please I beg you. Let them go. They're too young—

No two hands can forever hold each other.

What are you doing with that torch? No, don't, don't do that! Wait, wait, where are you taking my children. Stop, please, I beg you—

Once in uniform, a soldier never remembers the meaning of a mother's cry.

No, don't, don't. Not my baby, not the unborn—

If red were the smell of something, it would be the smell of charred bones, the smell of knowing that nobody was spared.

On the day of the mosque, red is a forbidden color.

All color is forbidden. White is as pure as the burnt house of the unborn.

x. The child

The child bathes in sunlight. He shivers as in the mornings when his
mother used to pour water over his head. He thinks that maybe
sunlight can be boiled like water at dawn.

Everything about the morning is cold.

The wind blows. The twigs slightly shake above him. His shadow
moves, and only then does he start thinking of what was.

He wishes he could feel the walls of the house again, find between the
bamboo cracks the marbles he hid from his mother.

The marble holes on the ground are now covered with soil. The bullet
holes on the walls are not. The sun comes through the holes in the
morning, and the moon at night. They roll and bounce on the
floor.

The part of the chicken he liked most was the wings. He hasn't eaten
for weeks; there is no need to. He always wished he could fly.

The older boys taught him how to leap over big rocks. The bubble
taught him how to float over them.

The eyes of fish, which he saved for last, were the best part of his
meal. He would lose them in a plate of rice but he could tell them
apart in his mouth. Now, he swims with fish, talks to fish.

The bubble taught him the language of the sea.

For the village children, there are two sides to life:
the days they eat and the nights they don't.
His mother never failed to feed him.

The other side of life for him was the nights
when his mother sang to him until he fell asleep.
The wind would brush against his hair
enough to turn his mother's voice into mountains and trees.

When his mother gazes up at the sky, he stands beside her and with
   the chill of the night, sends her the scent of his night breath.

He is always awake at night now, always waiting for everyone to
   sleep. He watches his mother make endless turns on her bed.

He tries to touch her, which is most difficult, because he knows
   as soon as he moves his hands toward her, she is suddenly out
   of reach.

He will stand by his mother as long as he dreams to kiss her once again.

But there is an end to everything.

Ends, however far, are always close.

xi. Mother and child

There is noise in the way she stares at his picture.

There is noise in the dots of sunlight on the floor.

My son, there will always be noise in our most silent space.

How much of it is the voice of the wind passing through the mouths
   of bullet holes around her?

How much of the wind are the voices of those who were once alive,
   those who perished without knowing it?

There are always whispers here, indistinguishable from the sound
   leaves make. She knows. Often, she hears her child but as soon as
   she turns to look for him, it's only the swing of the door left ajar,
   the scratches of chicken in soil, or the wind slipping into the
   house, and as quickly, slipping out.

The mother fills a bucket with soil, pours water in it, adds cement. For
   minutes, she mixes them with a stick, thinking of how she used to
   cook rice when her child was ill, the moments of endless stir to
   make sure it was moist, as soft as fire under the pot. Rice softens
   with water and gentleness.

She walks to the wall of bullets.

      It was Sunday when the soldiers came.
As always, they were in green, faded green,
the color of trees before a predicted monsoon.

She sticks her finger through one hole, blocking the light, pushing it
   out. If only she had done that: removed bullets from the child's
   insides by merely pushing light.

      The soldiers were known for drinking,
for ransacking the village for rice and fish.
The people would give them the last catch;
they knew bullets were faster than the act of refusal.
The sea was not always generous, never gave enough time
to replace what was given out.
Because when the soldiers came hungry,
the grumble of their stomachs was as fearful as the clamor
of their rifles cocking.

      They had wasted bullets on anything:
ones that moved, ones that didn't.

They had wasted their bullets on those who stood still
when asked for a loaf of bread.
Unlike food, their supply of bullets never ends.

Although she had nothing to give, she knows she never offered them
her child.

A mother in black is bereft of generosity.

She sticks her finger into the bucket and scoops up a mound of
cement. She slowly covers one hole, then flattens it with her palm.

She covers the first bullet hole. The first bullet wasn't the one that
hit him.

The mother wasn't home; she left the child to buy a light bulb.
The soldiers came and asked the child for something.
The child responded by saying there was no light in the house.

Where is your Mama?

There is no light in the house, sir—

*Go, get a chair, take the bulb out, you fool! What do you have in that
house—*

Nothing, no one, just me. . .

Then fix the light!

The child went back in.
He stood on the chair. He felt he was floating in the darkness
of the house when he reached for the bulb above him.

The mother covers another hole, then another.

The first shot came when the child loosened the bulb.
Then the air roared with bullets and screams.
Laughter of men.

The soldiers had left when she returned. An hour had passed.

The villagers were there: around the house,
on their knees, on the steps, leaning against the trees,
all of them looked fallen, tall plants stabbed
before their first bloom.

What she found:
the child on the floor, the chair on its side,
and the bulb in his palm, unbroken, soiled with blood.

Mama, I'm thirsty…

In her hand was the bulb to replace it.
In front of her, what could never be replaced.

There has not been light in the house since. Only the candles that melt
    with the days.

Every day, she waters his grave as if she has just planted a seed.

She falls on her knees. The weight of darkness is as heavy as memory.

Covered bullet holes do not remove memories. Water does not make a
    dead seed grow.

The child appears in the dark. The bubble circles him.

She doesn't see him but she tells him, Forgive me for leaving you
    behind.

The child crawls toward his mother, his face is as bright as light, as open as the sky that awaits him.

Mama... I'm thirsty.

The mother finds the bulb in a drawer. She pulls a chair to the middle of the room.

The child runs back to the wall. The bubble follows him.

Mama, don't! They will shoot you!

In darkness, he hears nothing, just like before: it was so still, as if the whole village was praying in a procession of candles, so still, until the first bullet hit the wall.

The house is splashed with light. The sky opens wider.

Mama!

Come. We must go now. The bubble speaks.

Why?... No... My Mama...

It is finished.

The wind lifts the child over the mother who is kneeling on the floor, elbows on the chair, eyes on the bulb.

Mama!

Child, this is your mother.

The bubble thins.

The many faces on its surface slowly vanish.

The child vanishes into the light.

The light opens the mother's eyes.

Woman, this is your country.

Notes

"The Gods We Worship Live Next Door" is taken from a poem of the same title by Filipino-American poet and novelist Bienvenido Santos. The poem was published in *The Literary Review,* special issue on Philippine literature, edited by Leonard Casper, 1960. Five lines were reprinted by permission of Tomas N. Santos, literary executor of the works of Bienvenido N. Santos.

Five lines from "Dedication" by Czeslaw Milosz from *The Collected Poems: 1931–1987.* Copyright 1988 by Czeslaw Milosz Royalties, Inc. Reprinted by permission of HarperCollins Publishers.

"Filipineza," "Singapore Sunday," "Amsterdam Canal," and
"A Night in Dubai"
"Overseas Filipinos workers (OFWs), estimated at five million, sent a total of 4.832 billion dollars to their families in the Philippines from January to August, up 22.6 percent from 3.94 billion dollars in the same period last year, data from the Bangko Sentral ng Pilipinas (BSP) showed Friday.

"The dollar inflows from OFWs boosted the income account in the Philippines' balance of payments in January-August to a surplus of 2.906 billion dollars, up by 54.5 percent from the same period last year."—*Philippine Daily Inquirer,* November 22, 2002

The epigraph in "A Night in Dubai" is taken from a poem, "Face Lost in the Wilderness" by Fadwa Tuquan (translated by Naomi Shihab Nye). A major voice for the Palestinians, Tuquan is one of the most important writers in the Arab world. The poem can be found in *Against Forgetting: Twentieth Century Poetry of Witness,* edited by Carolyn Forché, Norton, 1993, p. 537.

"Azúcar"
"[Sugar] is a bitterweet contribution to the islands—yielding immense profits for a few plantation owners at the expense of workers who labored under conditions close to bondage. The sugar-producing areas of Luzon and Visayas

remain to this day a landscape of stark gaps between wealth and poverty, a fertile breeding ground for Communist insurgents promising radical change." Stanley Karnow, *In Our Image: America's Empire in the Philippines*, Ballantine Books, 1989, p. 60.

"To the Person Sitting in Darkness"
The quote is taken from Mark Twain's "To the Person Sitting in Darkness," *North American Review*, February 1901.

"1899: The Forgotten Leaf"
The epigraph is "from the letter of an American soldier-lad in the Philippines to his mother, published in Public Opinion, of Decorah, Iowa, describing the finish of a victorious battle." It is also taken from Mark Twain's "To the Person Sitting in Darkness," *North American Review*, February 1901.

"Consummatum Est"
Jose P. Rizal was an American-sponsored national hero, recommended by Gov. Gen. W. H. Taft to shift the Filipino attention from American colonization back to the horrors of Spanish empire. Ironically Rizal, who hailed from wealthy *Ilustrados,* allegedly chose to say "Consummatum Est," Latin for "it is finished," for his cryptic last words before being shot by a firing squad in 1896. These were also the last words of Jesus Christ on the cross, according to John 19:30.

"Sultan Kudarat"
"Government troops have admitted committing human rights violations following military operations against the New Peoples Army (NPA) in sitios Bucay-eel and Tacol of Sinapulan village here last March 11. In an April 6 dialog initiated by the Labugal Tribal Organization here, the Army official who led the operation admitted the military's error before the Commission on Human Rights (CHR) Regional Director, Attorney Ceriaco Jabido, National Commission on Indigenous People (NCIP) representatives, church officials, and villagers. Held at Sinapulan barangay hall, the dialog started at 10 am and continued without a lunch break until 2 pm. The villagers had accused the military of human rights violation after their houses were

destroyed, chickens butchered, kitchenware stolen, fishponds drained, a house hit by splinters from a howitzer, personal effects, guns, and a can of rice seeds taken." *Cyberdyaryo*, April 2002

"GI Baby"
"GI Baby" is a term used to describe children of American soldiers and their Filipino barmaids.

"Also known as 'Children of the Dust,' Amerasians were born out of relationships between American military servicemen or personnel and Filipino women from 1941 to August 1993.
    "When the U.S. bases closed down, they left between 20,000 to 50,000 fatherless children mostly living in poverty and deprivation in the Philippines." Rita Villadiego, *Philippine News*, September 2003

Tamura Ryuichi is an anti-militarist Japanese poet and founder of "The Waste Land," a group of Japanese modernists inspired by T. S. Eliot. The poem "Standing Coffin" can be found in *Against Forgetting: Twentieth Century Poetry of Witness*, edited by Carolyn Forché, Norton, 1993, p. 333.

"1942: The War Haiku"
After more than three hundred years of colonial rule, the Philippines finally gained its independence in 1946. Manila was among the cities most damaged during World War II. The poem is also dedicated to Filipino guerillas during the Japanese occupation.

"Japayuki"
"According to the Philippine Overseas Employment Administration, the Philippines sends annually an average of 70,000 entertainers to Japan. The Commission on Human Rights, however, was quoted that there are now 75,000 Filipinas in Japan working as dancers, entertainers, and commercial sex workers.
    "Filipina entertainers in the Japanese nightclub industry may be classified into two categories—those working under a six-month contract, and the arubaito system." *Visayan Daily Star*, December 2003.

"With the hoopla over the death of a Japayuki, Maricris Sioson, who died of a fatal kind of hepatitis aggravated by alcohol and drugs in a government-run provincial hospital, Japan requested the Philippine government to start phasing out the deployment of the Japayukis to Japan. However, instead of heeding even the request of legitimate agents of Filipino performers versus the 'entertainers,' the Philippine government simply raised the age of the Japayukis to 23 in accordance with Japan's Child Welfare Law and Anti-Child Prostitution Law after discovering that many Japayukis like Sioson had worked in Japan since they were at such tender age of 12 or 13." *Malaya*, January 2005.

"Queen"
Smokey Mountain is a garbage dump in the Tondo section of Manila where people, mostly children, scavenge for food, scraps, tin cans, metal, and bottles to sell to brokers.

"Brownout"
Brownouts in Philippine cities are scheduled regularly to save energy. On the evenings of brownouts, the old and the young gather to share mythical "horror stories," often about women in various stages of mutilation (e.g. *manananggal*).

"Witness"
The epigraph is taken from "Curfew" by Chilean poet Teresa de Jesus (a pseudonym), translated by Maria Proser, Arlene Scully, and James Scully. The poem can be found in *Against Forgetting: Twentieth Century Poetry of Witness*, edited by Carolyn Forché, Norton, 1993, p. 618.

"Find Me"
"The bodies of at least 160 people have been recovered after a huge mountain of rain-soaked garbage collapsed on a shantytown last week near Manila, Philippines, according to authorities.

"About 150 more people are missing and feared buried under the garbage, which collapsed Monday on an area known as Payatas in Quezon City in metropolitan Manila. Heavy rain and the stench of garbage and decomposing bodies have hampered retrieval operations, Red Cross spokeswoman Tessie Usapdin said Saturday." CNN, July 16, 2000.

"The Gods We Worship Live Next Door"
"Attempts to revive peace talks with Muslim separatists in Mindanao made little progress following a military offensive, which sparked mass displacement of civilians and increased tension related to alleged Islamist 'terrorist' bombings. Arbitrary arrests, torture, extrajudicial executions and 'disappearances' were reported in the context of operations against suspected Islamist 'terrorists,' Muslim separatists, and communist insurgents. Weaknesses in the criminal justice system made criminal suspects, including women and children, vulnerable to ill-treatment or torture and denial of fair trial safeguards. A moratorium on executions for convicted kidnappers and drug traffickers was lifted. Armed opposition groups were responsible for abuses, including killings and hostage-taking." Amnesty International 2004. (http://www.amnesty.org/)

"The issue of terrorism in the Philippines should be dealt with not from the perspective of Manila-Washington ties but from a serious study of how terrorism figures in the minds of leaders and armed men belonging to the large but deeply factionalized guerilla movements in the country. Terrorism can never be dissociated from guerilla warfare and the separatist movement in Mindanao. From these movements would arise religious extremists or millenarian groups. With the right resources and the right agenda, these movements will continue to attract men—skilled, intelligent, and experienced—who will come to grasp the practical realities of waging a war with a minimum of resources and maximum public impact." Marites Vitug and Glenda M. Gloria, *Under the Crescent Moon: Rebellion in Mindanao*, Ateneo 2000, p. 244.

Acknowledgments

Acknowledgment is made to the following journals, on-line magazines, and anthologies for poems which first appeared in them, some in slightly different versions.

The Asian Pacific American Journal: "1899: The Forgotten Leaf"

Bold Type Magazine (Random House Magazine On-line): "Pantoum: The Comfort Woman"

Borderlands: Texas Poetry Review: "GI Baby"

Del Sol Review: "Because Yesterday I Jumped Out of a Plane"

The Kenyon Review: "A Night in Dubai"

The Literary Review: "Azúcar," "Brownout," "Cycles," "Discovery of Skin," "Procession," "Singapore Sunday"

Mānoa: Pacific Journal of International Literature: "Glue Children" (published as "Streets of Manila, 1995")

Mid-American Review: "Japayuki"

Mockingbird: "Flower Vendor" (published as "White Flowers")

The Nation: "Filipineza"

New Letters: "Witness"

The NuyorAsian Anthology: "1942: The War Haiku" (published as "1946:8 Haiku")

Puerto del Sol: "Consummatum Est"

Snail's Pace Review: "Queen"

Screaming Monkeys: Critiques of Asian American Images: "Four Million" ("Singapore Sunday," "Amsterdam Canal," "A Night in Dubai," and "Filipineza")

Webdelsol and *The Literary Review:* "Azúcar," "Brownout," "Cycles," "Discovery of Skin," "Lunar Eclipse," "Procession," "Sultan Kudarat," "Singapore Sunday," "Flower Vendor" (published as "White Flowers"), and "The Gods We Worship Live Next Door" (published as "The Listening Eye").

"Pantoum: The Comfort Woman" also appeared in Poetry Society of America's award-winning poems booklet as recipient of the 1998 Lucille Medwick Memorial Award. These poems have also been published in the Philippines in *The Evening Paper, Likhaan Anthologies of the University of the Philippines, Father Poems Anthology, Philippine Free Press,* and *Philippine Graphic.*

A BIG THANKS TO EVERYONE whose loving support made this book possible—MARAMING SALAMAT!

Maraming salamat sa inyong lahat! Maraming salamat.